Go-Go Green Chile Recipes

By Lawrence J. Clark

Live Well. Eat Well. Be Happy!

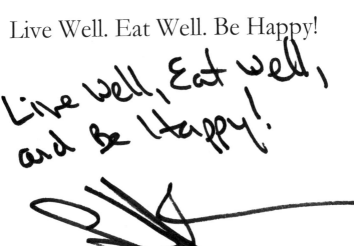

Live Well, Eat well, and Be Happy!

Published by American Mutt Press, a division of The Communication Leader, LLC.

Images courtesy of Lawrence J. Clark.

AMERICAN MUTT PRESS
Copyright © 2016

ISBN-13: 978-1540836083
ISBN-10: 1540836088

Order extra spice mixes today at: http://mountainmangourmet.com!

Did you know?

The chile pepper is
New Mexico's state vegetable!

Table of Contents

BREAKFAST

LUNCH

DINNER

NOTE: Unlike dried herbs and spices, green chile powder is made from a dried fruit product and must be heated to 165 degrees before consuming.

Download your FREE digital version of this book at:

http://mountainmangourmet.com/gggc4svedc/

Use the special code GGGC25OFF to receive a **25% discount** off your first order at MountainManGourmet.com!

About Lawrence J. Clark,
Your Mountain Man Gourmet

Lawrence J. Clark, aka the "Mountain Man Gourmet," began his love affair with food in early childhood. He has fond memories of swiping a fresh tomato off the kitchen counter and eating it like an apple, the juices running down his face and staining his shirt as he savored the luscious, nutritious fruit of the vine.

As an adult, Lawrence loves the way food smells as it's cooking on the stove or roasting or baking in the oven or sizzling on the grill. He loves the way it looks as it's growing on a tree or a bush or a plant in his garden. He loves the way it feels in his hands as he's cutting or grinding it or mixing it or stuffing it in his mouth. He loves the way it feels and tastes as he's chewing it and swallowing it and feeling it wind its way down into his stomach, especially a hot bowl of soup or a baked potato or a cup of Mountain Man Gourmet New Mexico Hot Chocolate on a chilly winter evening.

Lawrence is a veteran of the food and hospitality industry, having worked in fourteen restaurants and resort hotels in six different states from Maine to Mississippi to Florida while developing his career as a writer, educator, and musician. He has spent a lifetime traveling to over 40 states and 25 countries, where he's tasted a wide variety of cuisines and learned some fascinating new cooking techniques that he loves to pass along.

He enjoys spending time in his cabin in New Mexico's Manzano Mountains, and sharing his love of life and food on his Web-based cooking show and on various social media platforms.

You're welcome to find Lawrence online at MountainManGourmet.com, where you can enroll in a free membership to receive recipes, cooking tips, and instructional videos, as well as Facebook, Instagram, Pinterest, Twitter, YouTube, and more.

What the Heck is a
New Mexico Green Chile?

Based on its popularity and its prevalence in New Mexico's culture, one would think the Green Chile has been around for thousands of years, but that's not actually the case. In fact, the New Mexico chile was initially developed in 1894 by Dr. Fabián Garcia, a horticulturist at New Mexico State University.

Garcia started with 14 lineages of Pasilla, Colorado, and Negro cultivars that he found growing in New Mexico and Southern Colorado. These peppers were chosen because they had a "larger smoother, fleshier, more tapering and shoulderless pod for canning purposes."

His first chile was released in 1913, and was named "New Mexico No. 9."

Chile grown in the Hatch Valley, in and around Hatch, New Mexico, is called "Hatch Chile," but New Mexico Chile Peppers also grow along the entire Rio Grande River from northern Taos Pueblo to southern Isleta Pueblo. They are an important crop to New Mexico's economy and culture.

The New Mexico Green Chile pepper flavor is lightly pungent with a subtly sweet, spicy, smoky flavor. Not all Hatch chiles are the same variety, and the degree of "heat" or spiciness depends on the variety of New Mexico chile peppers that each farmer grows.

Chile peppers are also an excellent source of vitamins, including A, B, and C, and are high in fiber, phytonutrients, and Capsaicin, which some researchers claim can help prevent cancer. Chiles are also good for your metabolism, because Capsaicin's effect is similar to green tea (ECCG) in that it can help with weight loss. Capsaicin is also used to treat arthritis, shingles, nerve damage, and migraines.

Mountain Man Gourmet proudly uses only 100% Hatch Red and Green Chiles in our spice blends and other products.

*The official
New Mexico state question
is "Red or Green?"*

SNACKS & APPETIZERS

Go-Go Green Chile Deviled Eggs

What You Need:

- 12 fresh eggs
- 1/3 cup mayonnaise
- 4 bacon strips, cooked and crumbled
- 1 teaspoon Go-Go Green Chile mixed with 1 teaspoon boiling water*
- 1/4 teaspoon paprika

What to Do:

- Bring 12 eggs to a boil (use a pan big enough so they all lay flat on the bottom).

- While eggs are cooking, Cook 4 bacon strips until they are very crisp.

- Drain fat, then arrange bacon on a paper towel covered plate, let cool.

- After eggs are done, cool in ice water for a few minutes, then peel and rinse them.

- Slice eggs in half.

- Carefully remove the yolks and place in a large mixing bowl.

- Rinse egg whites under cool water, then arrange them on a platter.

- Mix Go-Go Green Chile with boiling water to form a paste.*

- Mash egg yolks with a fork. Blend in mayonnaise, crumbled bacon, and Go-Go Green Chile paste*.

- Using a spoon, scoop yolk mixture into each egg white.

- Sprinkle paprika on top of eggs before serving.

I like to munch on these mouth-watering delicacies while they're still slightly warm, but if you're not going to serve them right away, cover and refrigerate until ready to serve. Enjoy!

Green Chile Eggnog

WARNING: This is not your grandma's eggnog, but your guests will love this Southwestern take on the classic holiday favorite!

What You Need:

- 1 cup white or organic natural sugar
- 1/3 cup all-purpose flour
- 2 quarts whole milk
- 4 egg yolks
- 4 egg whites
- 4 extra teaspoons white sugar
- 2 teaspoons vanilla extract
- 1 teaspoon Mountain Man Gourmet Pure Hatch Green Chile Powder*
- 1 pinch ground nutmeg
- 1 cup whipped cream

- Cinnamon sticks or ground cinnamon

What to Do:

1. In a large saucepan, stir together the flour and one cup sugar.

2. Gradually stir in the milk, then bring the mixture to a boil over medium heat.

3. Whisk the egg yolks in a separate bowl until smooth.

4. Ladle a small amount of the hot milk into the yolks and quickly whisk in.

5. Next, very slowly (you don't want to make scrambled eggs!) pour the tempered yolk mixture back into the hot milk.

6. Cook, stirring constantly, just until mixture comes to a boil.

7. Remove pan from the heat, stir in one teaspoon (more or less to taste) Mountain Man Gourmet 100% Pure Hatch Green Chile Powder, and allow to cool.

8. While the milk/sugar/egg yolk mixture is cooling, place the egg whites in a separate bowl (a refrigerated glass or metal bowl

works best), then beat the egg whites with a wire whisk until foamy.

9. Gradually add 4 teaspoons sugar, continuing to beat until stiff peaks form.

10. Fold whites into the eggnog and refrigerate until chilled. Serve garnished with a dollop of whipped cream and a dash of nutmeg.

NOTE: If you are really adventurous (or really ugly and want to look better in your date's eyes) pour in a shot of tequila, vodka, or brandy just before serving.

*Unlike dried herbs and spices, green chile powder is made from a dried fruit product and must be heated to 165 degrees before consuming.

Go-Go Green Chile
Baked Sweet Potato Chips

One thing I've learned is that it takes more than a little trial and error to achieve that perfect crispy texture when making baked potato chips in the oven. Without that wonderful crunchy exterior, you're often left with the equivalent of a thinly sliced baked potato. Although it might taste delicious, it just doesn't deliver that satisfying crunch you've been craving.

Well, the good news is I have good news for you! The following recipe will help you achieve the results you want. The tradeoff is it takes a little while to happen, so be sure to allow plenty of time for this one. It can take up to 2 hours from start to finish, but the results are most definitely worth it. And you're going to love the juxta-position of the sweetness of the chips with the extra zip provided by the **Mountain Man Gourmet Go-Go Green Chile!**

NOTE: For best results, use a mandolin (special type of slicer) to achieve uniformly thin slices. If you don't have one, you can also use a sharp knife or vegetable peeler.

Here's What You'll Need:

- Corn or Canola Oil
- 2 large sweet potatoes, washed and peeled
- Mountain Man Gourmet Go-Go Green Chile, to taste

Other Stuff You'll Need:

- Mandolin slicer (preferably—see below for links to my favorite slicers)
- Parchment paper

How to Make Them:

1. First, preheat the oven to 250 degrees.
2. Using a mandolin, knife, or vegetable peeler, cut sweet potatoes into 1/8" inch thick slices. Place on parchment paper or clean kitchen towel to absorb excess moisture and set aside. Line 2 large, rimmed baking sheets with parchment paper.

Lightly coat surface with oil or cooking spray, then arrange sweet potato slices in a single layer on top. Sprinkle with Mountain Man Gourmet Go-Go Green Chile.

3. Place baking sheets in oven for one hour, then remove sheets and flip each chip. Sprinkle with additional Mountain Man Gourmet Go-Go Green Chile, if desired.

4. Return pans to oven (HINT: rotate each sheet and place on a different rack than before; for example, place the sheet that was on the top rack on the bottom rack and vice-versa).

5. Check on chips after 20 minutes. If they are not yet crispy, continue baking until they become crisp and golden brown. (BE PATIENT: The total baking time will vary by oven and the altitude where you live, as well as how much moisture is in your sweet potatoes. They should be ready within another 20 – 30 minutes).

6. Remove from oven and cool for a few minutes before serving. Once cool, store excess in an airtight container. Of course, that's assuming there are any chips leftover!

Need a mandolin slicer? Check out these two inexpensive hand-held models you can order from Amazon.com:

- OXO Good Grips Adjustable Hand Held Mandolin Slicer (large) http://amzn.to/2iNCo3u

- OXO Good Grips Adjustable Hand Held Mandolin Slicer (handheld) http://amzn.to/2hCAvGK

Or try this stand-up version, which includes two different Julienne slicer blades!

- Dynamic Chef Mandolin Slicer http://amzn.to/2izEroL

Or this one, which comes with a French fry blade as well!

- VonShef 'V' Shaped Multi Slicer with 5 Blades http://amzn.to/2hMiZLq

Crusty Go-Go
Green Chile Bread

Yields: 2 loaves (cut recipe in half for single loaf)

What You'll Need For the Bread Dough:

- 6c unbleached all-purpose flour
- 2 t. yeast
- 1 t. salt
- 3 T. Go-Go Green Chile Spice Blend
- 3 cups warm water (not boiling, as that will kill the yeast)

Special Equipment

- Dutch Oven (I use a Lodge 5-Quart Pre-Seasoned Cast-Iron Dutch Oven with

<u>Dual Handles</u>. To order yours go to
http://amzn.to/2iNQbXU)

How to Prepare

1. Whisk together flour, salt, Go-Go Green Chile, and yeast in a large bowl.

2. Add water and stir until all ingredients are blended (dough will be loose and sticky).

3. Cover bowl with plastic wrap and set in a warm, draft-free area overnight, or for about 12 - 18 hours (don't worry, you can keep it up to 24 hours before cooking).

4. Preheat oven to 450 degrees.

5. Place an empty cast iron Dutch oven (with lid) in the oven and heat it for 30 minutes.

6. While waiting for the Dutch oven to heat up, dump half of the risen dough onto a heavily floured surface and lightly shape into a round loaf.

HINT: Dip hands in flour to prevent dough from sticking to your fingers.

7. Carefully remove hot Dutch oven from the oven and place the dough inside.

8. Cover and return to oven for 30 minutes.

9. Remove the lid and bake for about 10-15 more minutes.

10. Remove bread from oven and let cool for 15-30 minutes on a wire cooling rack.

11. For second loaf, reheat Dutch oven for 30 minutes and repeat the process outlined above, or purchase a second Dutch oven here: http://amzn.to/2iNQbXU.

Enjoy with your favorite soup, stew, or salad!

Go-Go Green Chile Baked Chicken Wings

This recipe is my take on the old "Shake 'N Bake" meals my mom used to prepare back in the 1960s and 70s. Since the chicken "fries" itself while baking in the oven, there's no need to add a bunch of extra oil, and by dusting the wings with bread crumbs during cooking, there's no need to do the "Shake" before the "Bake."

Say hello to your favorite new, healthy (well, um, healthier) chicken wing!

What You'll Need

- 1 Package (about 4-5 pounds) fresh whole chicken wings
- 2 T. Go-Go Green Chile Spice Blend
- 1-2 cups plain breadcrumbs (I mix mine half and half with Panko crumbs)

- Celery and Carrots for garnish

How to Prepare

1. Pre-heat oven to 400 degrees.
2. Spread chicken wings in a single layer on a foil-covered baking sheet. Spread each wing out fully so it lies as flat as possible.
3. Sprinkle liberally with Go-Go Green Chile and a light dusting of plain bread crumbs.
4. Cook for 20 minutes.
5. Remove from oven and, using tongs, flip wings over.
6. Sprinkle with more Go-Go Green Chile and bread crumbs.
7. Cook for 20 minutes.
8. Remove from oven and, using tongs, flip wings over again.
9. Sprinkle with more Go-Go Green Chile and bread crumbs.
10. Cook for 10 minutes.
11. Repeat process until desired crispness is achieved.

Serve with celery, carrots, and a bowl of Go-Go Green Chile Sauce for dipping (see recipe).

BREAKFAST

Christmas Breakfast Skillet

Ok, so it's Christmas morning—you wake up early, the kids are tearing through the wrapping paper, everybody's havin' a good ole time, but then your stomach starts to grumble.

What to do?

Shop at Amazon.com!

Well, I guess you could, but even with one-day shipping the whole clan would be clamoring for their breakfast way before it got there.

And you don't want to ask your wife to cook something, because since you were such a cheapskate on her presents last year you're trying to be extra nice this morning to make up for it.

Pancakes? Frozen waffles?

Nah . . . this is a special day, and you need to make something festive and decorative for the occasion. I know—how about cooking up a batch of Mountain Man Gourmet Christmas Skillet Breakfast?

Here's the quick and easy recipe:

What You Need For the Skillet:

- 2 Russet Potatoes
- 2 Sweet Potatoes (Yams)
- ½ Bermuda (Red) Onion
- 2-3 cloves fresh or 1 tbsp. chopped garlic
- 1 Avocado
- 2 Roma Tomatoes
- 5-6 Fresh Eggs

What to Do:

1. In a large skillet (I use a Lodge 12" Pre-Seasoned Cast Iron Skillet) slowly brown equal parts of chopped up sweet potatoes and russet potatoes in some canola or corn oil. You can also add a little butter for extra

flavor, but wait until they are about halfway done to avoid burning the butter.

2. Brown the potatoes SLOWLY and stir often for even cooking and that tasty, crunchy exterior we all know and love.

3. When the potatoes are about 3/4 done, toss in some chopped Bermuda (red) onion and garlic, then sprinkle on some Mountain Man Gourmet Go-Go Green Chile spice blend. If you're out, no problem — you can always order more at: http://mountainmangourmet.com.

4. Stir a few times and cook for a while longer, then toss in some sliced mushrooms.

5. After the mushrooms are slightly cooked, add a few slices of fresh tomato.

6. Next, drop five or six whole eggs in the pan, scattering them around so the yolks don't touch.

7. If you like, sprinkle some more Go-Go Green Chile over the eggs.

8. Shred or slice up some cheddar cheese (I love Cabot's extra sharp cheddar) and scatter some around as well.

9. Add a few slices of fresh avocado. Now that you've added the fresh tomato slices (red) and avocado (green), see why this is a Christmas recipe?

10. Turn heat down to low and cover for a while (time depends on whether you like your eggs to be golden and runny or cooked to death until they taste like cardboard). Be sure to leave the lid slightly open or use a skillet splatter screen, or you'll lose that tasty crunch you worked so hard to get on the potatoes.

11. Final step: Serve it to the family and listen to the raves!

NOTE: This is an especially good recipe for your teenage daughter who just announced she has joined PETA and become a vegetarian. (Don't worry, she'll change her mind when she smells the Christmas T-Bones smoking on the grill later.)

Green Chile Banana Bread

(Makes 2 loaves.)

One of my favorite breakfast foods is a thick, toasted slice of banana bread, with or without a healthy slab of real butter melting over the top.

This recipe can be followed without adding the green chile powder, but this one simple addition gives it just that added boost of flavor to get you off to a great start in the morning—try with a cup of hot, steaming Mountain Man Gourmet New Mexico Hot Chocolate!

What You'll Need

Food Items
- 6 bananas (the riper the better)
- 2 eggs
- 3/4 C. melted unsalted butter

- 1 C. brown sugar
- 1 T. vanilla
- 3 C. flour (I use 1/2 white and 1/2 whole wheat)
- 2 T. baking soda
- 1/4 t. salt
- 1 T. 100% Pure Green Chile Powder

How to Make It

1. Preheat Oven to 350 F.
2. Grease a Loaf Pan with butter, oil or cooking spray.
3. Mash Bananas with fork in a large mixing bowl.
4. Melt Butter in a small saucepan.
5. Combine wet ingredients and sugar; mix with bananas until well combined.
6. Mix dry ingredients in a separate bowl.
7. Combine wet and dry ingredients, stir just until well combined.

8. Divide batter into 2 loaf pans, then bake in 350 degree oven for 50-60 minutes. (Loaf is done when a toothpick inserted in the center comes out clean).

Allow to cool on a wire rack, then slice and serve. Freeze one loaf for a healthy treat later in a few weeks or months!

Go-Go Green Chile
Potato Pancakes

(Makes 4 servings.)

What You'll Need

- 2 C. leftover mashed potatoes
- 2 eggs
- ¼ C. bread crumbs
- 2 T. Go-Go Green Chile Spice Blend
- 2 T. olive oil
- 2 tomatoes

How to Make Them

1. Whisk mashed potatoes, eggs, and Go-Go Green Chile together, then form into ½ inch thick patties.

2. Coat with bread crumbs.

3. Fry in olive oil for 2-3 minutes per side, until golden brown.

4. Drain excessive oil by placing cooked patties on a paper towel-covered plate.

5. Place in 200 degree oven to keep warm until ready to serve; you can also refrigerate or freeze, then heat them in oven or on stove top whenever you're in the mood for one (or two or three or four).

Serve with fresh tomato slices and fried eggs (I like to cook them over easy, so the yolks are runny enough to soak up with crispy bites of the potato pancakes—yum!).

Optional: crumble up bacon, sausage, or ham and mix with potatoes before cooking.

Easy, Mouth-Watering Homemade Biscuits

(Makes about 1 dozen biscuits. NOTE: This recipe is for "regular" buttermilk biscuits, so if you want to make plain biscuits, follow the instructions below. See "variation" note at end for making Go-Go Green Chile Biscuits. So now you have two recipes for the price of one. Pretty good deal, eh?)

What You'll Need

- 2 1/2 C. unbleached all-purpose flour (I use Hungarian High Altitude Unbleached Flour, but you can experiment with different types)

- 3/8 t. baking soda

- 4 t. baking powder (use one without aluminum)

- 1 t. sea salt

- 1 C. buttermilk

- 4 oz. (8 T.) unsalted butter, chilled

How to Make Them

1. First, preheat oven to 450°F.

2. Next, thoroughly mix 2 cups flour, salt, baking soda, and baking powder in a large bowl.

3. Combine the dry ingredients in a bowl, or in the bowl of a food processor.

4. Chop the chilled butter into small chunks, dump into the flour bowl, then squeeze butter with your fingers—keeping going until butter is reduced to small, pebble-like granules.

5. Add buttermilk and mix until all flour is absorbed—for fluffier biscuits, do not overmix—dough should be wet and sticky at this point..

6. Dump the dough out onto a board covered with a thin coating of flour.

7. Starting in the middle, press down dough with your palms. Keeping working your way out to the edges until you get one large flat piece of dough about 1.2" thick.

8. Next, fold the dough in half, then half again, and press down with palms. Turn and repeat 6-8 times, then spread out the dough with your palms until it's ½-1" thick (thicker dough will rise more but will take a bit longer to cook).

9. Use a juice or rocks glass, biscuit cutter, or cookie cutter to form biscuits.

10. Place the biscuits on a flat sheet pan (I cover mine with foil for easy cleanup—place foil dull side up). If you prefer softer edges, bunch biscuits together in center of pan so edges are touching each other. For crispier edges, place biscuits about 1 inch apart.

11. Bake for about 8 minutes, then remove and quickly brush with melted butter.

12. Return biscuits to oven for about 3-4 more minutes and keep the door closed! Keep a close eye on them—you want them to be slightly golden brown but not burned.

Biscuits are done when you hear a hollow sound while tapping on them with a spoon.

Variation: Omit salt and add 2 tablespoons Mountain Man Gourmet Go-Go Green Chile Spice Blend while mixing dry ingredients.

Hint: Make a double batch, then freeze the leftovers, or freeze pre-cut, uncooked biscuits up to 6 weeks, then bake at 450°F for 15-20 minutes—at about 12-14 minutes, check progress and brush with melted butter.

LUNCH

Go-Go Green Chile Chicken Lettuce Wraps

Make this delicious, yet light chicken salad meal for lunch or a light dinner. For an even quicker meal, pick up a pre-cooked plain rotisserie chicken, season it with Go-Go Green Chile, then heat it up in the oven.

Feeds: 2-4 human adults, or a butt load of kids— double recipe for even more yumminess!

Total Prep Time: 20 minutes to prepare, plus time for flavors to combine

What You'll Need

Dressing:

- 1 T. REAL mayonnaise (not Miracle Whip)

- 2 T. Greek or Plain yogurt

- 2 t. Dijon mustard

- 1 t. garlic powder

- 1 t. dried oregano

- 1 T. Go-Go Green Chile Spice Blend

- (optional) 1-2 t. red wine vinegar or a few drops of balsamic vinegar

- salt and pepper, to taste

Chicken Salad:

- 3 stalks celery, finely chopped

- 3/4 C. pecans or walnuts, roughly chopped

- 3 T. fresh parsley, finely chopped (for a refreshing, tangier taste try Cilantro instead)

- 2 green onions, finely sliced (no green onions in the fridge? Substitute regular or Bermuda onion)

- **10-12 oz. pre-cooked boneless chicken thighs or breast** cooked with Go-Go Green Chile Spice Blend

- OR

- **10-12 oz. raw boneless chicken thighs or breast** and 2 Tbsp. Go-Go Green Chile Spice Blend

If using pre-cooked chicken: Sautee over medium heat in a tablespoon or two of olive oil until warmed through and a little crispy on the outside

If using raw chicken: Coat chicken liberally with Go-Go Green Chile, then sauté in olive oil in a cast-iron pan over medium-high heat until cooked thoroughly. Try charring the edges slightly to experience a fresh-grilled taste.

Chop cooked, reheated chicken into small cubes (about 1/2").

Wraps:

- 4-6 large Iceberg or Romaine lettuce leaves (Butterhead Lettuce (any variety, including Boston, Butter, and Bibb) also works great for this recipe because it has naturally bowl-shaped leaves.

- **Garnish (optional):** chopped fresh

parsley or cilantro

• Sliced green or red onions

How to Make Them:

1. In a small glass, stainless steel, or plastic mixing bowl, combine mayonnaise, yogurt, Dijon mustard, garlic powder, oregano, Add salt and pepper to taste, but remember the chicken will have plenty of flavor. Stir and combine thoroughly. Set aside.

2. In a larger bowl, combine chicken breast, celery, nuts, parsley or cilantro, and onion. Add dressing and gently stir to combine all ingredients thoroughly.

3. Cover and place in refrigerator for a minimum of 30 minutes; for even better flavor, leave overnight.

4. To serve, scoop portions of chicken salad into lettuce leaves. Garnish with parsley, cilantro and/or green or red onions.

   5. Serve immediately and chow down!

Extra Crunchy Green Chile Fish Tacos

Ok, guys—here's a simple but great-tasting recipe that you can cook for a quiet weekend lunch at home with your honey, or for a houseful of guys watching the next big game.

One of my wife's favorite dishes is fish tacos; whenever we go to a restaurant where they are served, I can count on her ordering them. Of course, this makes me happy because I usually get to taste some of hers. I rarely order them myself, though, because they are one food item that tastes great when done well, but is terribly disappointing when done poorly.

I have had some decent fish tacos, and I've had some terrible fish tacos. And when I say terrible, I mean awful. Gross. Disgusting. Pick your adjective and fill in the blank.

Soooo . . . here is my version of fish tacos, which I hope you will agree does not live up to any of the previously mentioned negative descriptions. I call my recipe "Extra Crunchy Green Chile Fish Tacos."

And the good news is you can easily make these delicious fish tacos right in your own kitchen!

What You Need for the Tacos

Tortillas: I'm far too lazy to make fresh tortillas, but most store-bought tortillas taste like cardboard. A good alternative is to buy tortillas that are half-cooked, then cook them the rest of the way at home. They only take about 20-30 seconds per side, and the difference in taste is HUGE.

Here is one brand I've found that is consistently good, and is sold in many of the major grocery chains: Guerrero® Tortillas de Harina Fresquiricas.

To prepare your tortillas beforehand, simply heat up a comal (flat cast iron griddle used in Mexican cooking) or cast iron frying pan, cook up a few tortillas, then place them in the oven in a covered dish so they'll stay warm until ready to serve.

Fish Taco Filling

- ½ pound fish per person (I like white, flaky fish, such as Cod or Haddock)
- Flour – mix of white, wheat, and cornmeal
- Very cold water, seltzer water, lemon-lime soda, or beer
- Mountain Man Gourmet Go-Go Green Chile Spice Blend
- Corn or Canola Oil

What To Do:

1. First, make the batter—mix equal parts flour (I use a third each of white, wheat, and corn flour) and VERY cold water (you can also use seltzer water or beer—just make sure it's very cold).

    a. While stirring the batter, keep adding liquid until you get a smooth consistency—not too thick, not too runny. It should stick easily to the fish when you dip it into the batter.

   b. Also mix in about 1 teaspoon Mountain Man Gourmet Go-Go Green Chile Spice Blend per ½ pound of fish (use more or less to taste).

2. Cut fish into rectangular chunks (about 1" X 2-3")

3. Dip fish into batter, shake off excess

4. Drop into medium-high oil (about 350-375 degrees)

5. Fry in Cast Iron Skillet until crispy, turn with metal tongs as needed

6. Now, here's the trick to make it "extra crunchy": pull each chunk of fish out of the pan (use tongs—its HOT!), dip it into the bowl of batter, then fry it again for a couple of minutes. I learned this trick from a Chinese chef in San Francisco. It works and tastes great with the extra crunch factor!

7. Drain cooked fish in colander or on absorbent cloth or paper towels, then keep warm on uncovered plate or sheet pan in oven.

What You Need for Lorenzo's Roasted Green Chile Salsa

While the fish is cooking, very thinly slice the following items:

- ¼ Cabbage

- ½ Onion (use Bermuda onion if possible, can also substitute shallots)

- 2-3 Fresh Roasted Peppers (Hatch Green Chile, Poblano, Anaheim, Jalapeno, etc. will work)

    o If fresh green chiles are out of season, or you are not lucky enough to live in New Mexico, I recommend purchasing frozen or canned Hatch Green Chiles.

- A few leaves of Fresh Basil

Mix the sliced veggies with some mayonnaise and a few drops of rice wine vinegar (more or less to taste).

NOTE: I like adding a spoonful of Mountain Man Gourmet Go-Go Green Chile spice blend to the mayo to give the sauce a little extra oomph. Remember, though, that green chile powder must be heated to 165 degrees before consuming, so simply mix equal parts of the powder with boiling water to form a paste, then cool and use as desired.

Ok, that's all there is to it...

Spread a healthy scoop of the salsa on the tortillas, drop a few chunks of cooked extra crunchy fish on each, top with a little extra salsa, and then serve it up. Don't forget to give thanks to the Lord for inventing fish (I always add an extra prayer of thanks for those who caught and cleaned them, as well).

Enjoy with your favorite wife and your favorite frosty, cold beverage!

Go-Go Green Chile
Turkey Spinach Burgers

Yes, this sounds like a weird combination, but it's actually quite tasty and a little healthier than the traditional beef burger. The sunflower seeds provide a hearty, crunchy texture, and the spinach add extra flavor in addition to some extra nutrition. And according to one of my all-time favorite cartoon characters, Popeye, it will also put hair on your chest!

You can serve it on a bun like a burger, or serve as a standalone patty in a traditional plated meal with a starch and veggies on the side. Try it smothered with Go-Go Green Chile Sauce (see recipe).

HINT: I like frying up leftover Go-Go Green Chile Turkey Spinach Burgers with some eggs and leftover rice for a quick and flavorful breakfast.

What You'll Need

- 12-16 oz. ground turkey
- ½ bunch fresh or 1 small box frozen spinach
- 2 eggs
- ½ C. diced onion
- ½ C. diced celery
- ¼ C. sunflower seeds, shelled
- 2 T. Go-Go Green Chile Spice Blend
- 1 t. garlic salt
- ½ t. black pepper
- Dry bread crumbs
- Cheddar cheese (optional)

What to Do

1. Wash and finely chop fresh spinach OR thaw and drain frozen spinach, squeezing out as much excess moisture as possible.

2. Mix the turkey, spinach, sunflower seeds, eggs, and seasonings together.

3. Add enough breadcrumbs so the mixture holds together.

4. Divide into patties.

HINT: Place turkey burger mixture between two sheets of waxed paper and flatten before dividing into patties.

5. Pan fry, bake, or grill patties until cooked through. If desired, top with cheese for last few minutes.

Serve on a bun with Mayo or Go-Go Green Chile Sauce (or both). If desired, add tradition burger toppings such as lettuce, tomato, pickles, etc.

DINNER

Cucumber Spaghetti with Fresh Pesto

This unique and easy to make low-carb dish is a great way to savor the naturally delicious flavors of fresh cucumber, basil, garlic, and toasted pine nuts. This dish makes a great entrée just by itself, or you can serve with your favorite protein, such as grilled chicken or steamed fish, for a more satisfying meal.

Unlike most of my recipes, this dish requires a fancy gadget (a spiral slicer, thankfully not very expensive—see Amazon links below) to create "spaghetti noodles" out of the cucumbers. Yeah, I know, cucumber spaghetti sounds *really weird*, but once you try this method, you're going to love it and you'll also have a lot of fun trying out the different shapes and sizes that you can make with the various attachments. This is also a great way to get the kids or grandkids involved in cooking! See below for links to a couple of my favorite spiral slicers.

NOTE: For best results use thick, seedless cucumbers.

Serves: 4 adults

Total Prep Time: 15-20 minutes

What You'll Need

Food Items:

- 4 large, firm seedless cucumbers, peeled
- ½ C. fresh pesto*

Special equipment: vegetable spiral slicer, such as the **Paderno World Cuisine Tri-Blade Vegetable Spiral Slicer** or the **OXO Spiral Vegetable Slicer**. Follow the links below to purchase from Amazon.com:

Paderno World Cuisine Tri-Blade Vegetable Spiral Slicer: http://amzn.to/2ilCrka OXO Spiral Vegetable Slicer: http://amzn.to/2ipQTdg

*See recipe for Mountain Man Gourmet Pesto

How to Make Your Cucumber Spaghetti:

1. Prepare Mountain Man Gourmet Go-Go Green Chile Fresh Basil Pesto. Using a spiral slicer, cut cucumbers into thick, long noodles. (If using the **Paderno Tri-Blade Vegetable Spiral Slicer**, use the medium "chipper" blade to create thicker strands).

2. Once they reach 10-12" long, cut the noodles with kitchen scissors. Place cut noodles on paper or clean kitchen towels and gently pat dry to absorb excess moisture.

3. Place cucumber noodles in a medium, non-reactive bowl (glass or plastic) and top with fresh pesto. Toss gently to combine. Season with salt and pepper, to taste, and serve immediately.

Herb-Encrusted Chicken with Tangy Lime Cream Sauce

What You'll Need for the Chicken

- 1 T. Dijon or coarsely ground mustard
- 1 T. olive oil
- Zest of 1 lime
- 1/2 t. dried or ½ T. fresh Thyme
- 1/2 t. dried or ½ T. fresh Rosemary
- Kosher salt and freshly ground black pepper, to taste
- 8 boneless chicken thighs or breasts (bone-in meats will always produce better flavor, but either will work fine for this recipe)
- 2 T. unsalted butter

What You'll Need for the Cream Sauce

- 1/2 cup water or chicken broth
- 1/2 cup heavy cream or half and half
- 2 cloves garlic, finely chopped
- 2 T. Go-Go Green Chile Spice Blend
- Juice of 1 lime
- 1/2 t. dried or ½ T. fresh Thyme
- 1/2 t. dried or ½ T. fresh Rosemary
- 1 t. dried or ½ T. fresh Basil
- Sea salt or Kosher salt and freshly ground black pepper

How to Prepare This Dish

1. Preheat oven to 375 degrees.

2. In a medium bowl, combine olive oil, mustard, lime zest, thyme, rosemary, and a few pinches of salt. Drop in chicken and turn several times to coat all sides.

3. Melt butter in a large cast iron skillet over medium high heat. Add chicken and sear both sides until outsides are golden brown, about 3-4 minutes per side (no, they're not fully cooked

yet, but that's ok). Remove chicken from pan and keep on a plate for now.

4. Add garlic and Hatch Red Chile to the skillet. Sautee for a couple of minutes; this is going to smell really great!

5. Stir in water or chicken broth, cream or half and half, lime juice, and herbs. Add salt and pepper to taste (the wonderful fragrant herbs and tangy lime can produce an excellent flavor without having to add too much salt).

6. Bring sauce to a boil, then reduce heat and simmer until slightly thickened.

7. Add chicken back to the skillet; turn several times to coat chicken evenly. You're almost there!

8. Place skillet into the oven for about 20-30 minutes or until cooked through. Be sure chicken reaches an internal temperature of 165 degrees to avoid any nasty foodborne illnesses.

9. Serve with rice, plain or buttered pasta, etc. Spoon excess cream sauce over chicken, then top with finely chopped Rosemary, Basil, and Thyme. Steamed broccoli or a leafy, dark green such as Kale makes an excellent side dish for this meal and helps to offset the richness of the sauce.

10. Eat with your favorite family members or guests, and get ready for a huge wave of compliments!

Oven-Blackened Salmon
with Crisp Veggies

What You Need:

- ½ pound of Salmon Fillets per person

- Unsalted butter

- Mountain Man Gourmet Go-Go Green Chile Spice Blend

- I like adding some extra garlic powder and dried, minced onion

- Assortment of crisp raw vegetables, such as:
    Carrots
    Celery
    Bell Pepper
    Sweet Vidalia or Red (Bermuda) Onion
    Tomato

What to Do:

Here's a quick and easy recipe that even my little brother can make. Of course, if he reads this, he's going to have a few comments, but he tried out my Extra Crunchy Green Chile Fish Tacos and said they came out pretty good, so let's see what he can do with this one . . .

1. First, get a baking dish and line it with foil. The foil isn't a must, but it sure makes it a heck of a lot easier to clean up later, which means more time to play my guitar or fiddle around with my other favorite instrument, the Wife. Yup, and she appreciates a few less minutes in the kitchen and the extra attention, too, if you get my drift.

2. Anyway, turn the oven on really hot, say about 425 to 430 degrees. Drop a couple of chunks of unsalted butter in the pan, along with a generous sprinkling of Mountain Man Gourmet Go-Go Green Chile. For this recipe, I like adding some extra garlic powder and dried, minced onion.

3. Place the baking dish in the oven for a few minutes, keeping a close eye on it. The point is to get the butter melted and bubbling, almost smoking, before you drop in the fish.

4. While the pan is heating up, chop up some crispy raw veggies, like carrots, celery, bell pepper, red (Bermuda) onion, etc. I also like to put some thick slices of tomato on the plate, as it gives some nice color and also sooths the tongue from the heavily seasoned fish.

5. Remember that unless you are making baked goods, or dealing with salt or hot peppers, the proportions and the shapes are not all that important. For this dish, I like to cut the veggies into big enough slices and chunks that they can be enjoyed individually, but not so big that they need to be cut again before eating.

6. Alrighty then . . . now that you've got the veggies cut and the butter melted, pull the pan out of the oven (careful—it will be really hot and might be smoking a bit, so you'll want to wear some oven mitts and also turn off the fire alarm

briefly, especially if you've got an ornery alarm like mine that starts beeping if I walk by it after going for a good hike around the ranch).

7. Drop the fish (cut in about fist-sized portions, 4-6 oz. each) into the pan; lay it down gently and away from you so it doesn't splatter. The idea here is to get the butter really hot, so you're simulating the heat generated by a frying pan, but with the even heat generated by an oven. That way the fish cooks on both sides, but the side that's touching the pan gets crispier.

8. Cook the fish for about 5-7 minutes, then remove the pan from the oven, flip the fish over, and cook for about 4-5 more minutes. Remember these times are just a guideline, as it all depends on how cold the fish was to start with, how thick it is cut, how well you like it cooked, etc. If the salmon is not done quite enough for your liking, you can always put it back in the oven for a few more minutes.

9. When you're ready to serve, place the salmon in the middle of the plate, then

arrange the veggies around it, alternating the colors so it looks nice. The women-folk appreciate that kind of stuff, and it might make up for whatever you did to get in the dog house earlier that day.

I like to serve this dish with some piping hot garlic bread, but you could also serve it over rice or some lightly buttered pasta–angel hair would be a good choice here.

Alrighty then . . . that's about all there is to it; hope you enjoy this tasty treat!

Go-Go Green Chile
Shrimp and Rice

Ingredients

- 1 onion, chopped
- 1 green bell pepper, chopped
- 2-3 fresh or 1 (15 oz.) can diced tomatoes
- 1 C. half and half
- 1 t. sugar
- 1 t. olive oil
- 2 T. Go-Go Green Chile Spice Blend
- 1 package (12-16 oz.) raw, deveined shrimp, thawed
- 2 C. cooked rice

Directions

1. Cook rice according to directions.

2. While rice is cooking, heat 1 T. olive oil in a large skillet.

3. Sautee onion and green pepper until tender. Stir in tomatoes, half and half, sugar, and Go-Go Green Chile. Mix well.

4. Stir in shrimp.

5. Cover and simmer over low heat for about 10 minutes or until hot and shrimp is cooked.

Serve over hot rice. A piping hot loaf of garlic bread also goes well with this meal!

SPICES, SAUCES & SEASONINGS

Go-Go Green Chile
Fresh Basil Pesto

You can enjoy this fresh, bold, flavorful pesto with your favorite pasta, fish, chicken, soup, or vegetable recipes. It also makes a great sandwich spread or pizza topping.

NOTE: You can make pesto with a food processor to combine the ingredients, but I recommend chopping the ingredients by hand for a more rustic, yet elegant finished product. Instead of ending up with a smooth "saucy" type pesto, you'll be able to taste the distinct individual flavors with each bite.

What You'll Need

- 2 C. fresh basil leaves
- ¼ C. toasted pine nuts (unsalted cashews also work well in this recipe)

LAWRENCE J. CLARK

- 2–3 garlic cloves
- 1/3 C. plus 2 T. extra virgin olive oil
- 2/3 C. Parmesan cheese, freshly grated
- 2 t. Mountain Man Gourmet Go-Go Green Chile, mixed with 2 t. very hot water
- Salt and pepper, to taste

How to Prepare the Pesto

1. Remove basil leaves from stems, then wash and pat dry.

2. Finely chop the basil and peeled garlic gloves.

3. Crush nuts with the bottom of a heavy glass or pan, or grind in a mortar and pestle or spice grinder.

4. Add all ingredients to a glass jar (leftover spaghetti sauce jars work great for this purpose), then add 1/3 cup extra virgin olive oil and shake until blended thoroughly.

5. Stir in Parmesan cheese and remaining olive oil until you've achieved the desired consistency. At this point, be sure to taste

your creation, then season with salt and pepper if needed.

IMPORTANT: Use immediately for best flavor. If desired, freeze leftovers in ice cube trays covered with a layer of olive oil. Once frozen, remove your "pesto cubes" from trays (trust me, you *don't* want one of these in your favorite Scotch on the rocks) and store them in freezer-safe plastic bags for future use. These cubes are excellent for use in soups or stews.

Homemade Go-Go Green Chile Taco Seasoning Mix

This tasty recipe takes just a few minutes to mix and costs much less than buying pre-packaged taco seasoning. It also has less salt, no artificial colors or flavors or preservatives, and tastes great, too!

NOTE: You can also buy pre-mixed Go-Go Taco Seasoning, as well as many other Mountain Man Gourmet products and gift baskets, at MountainManGourmet.com.

What You'll Need:

- 2 T. Mountain Man Gourmet 100% Pure Hatch Green Chile Powder
- 1 T. ground cumin
- 1 t. ground coriander
- 2 t. garlic powder

- 1 t. crushed red pepper flakes
- 2 t. smoked paprika
- 1 t. salt
- 2 t. black pepper

How to Prepare

1. Combine all ingredients in an airtight container and shake well to combine.

Yup, that's all you need to do!

You can also make this recipe in larger batches; store unused amounts in an air tight container for about 6 months. NOTE: It won't go bad, but will begin losing flavor after that point.

How to Use

Use 3 - 4 tablespoons per pound of ground beef, pork, chicken, or turkey (or any combination of the above—experiment and make up your own special meat blend!). For more even flavor, mix your taco seasoning with meat before cooking.

To really make your tacos "pop" with flavor, grind your spice mix down in a mortar and pestle or electric spice grinder just before using. This one small step makes an amazing difference in the taste!

Go-Go Green Chile Sauce

I love this bold and flavorful sauce, and it's become a staple in the Mountain Man Gourmet home. You can use it on Huevos Rancheros, Smothered Burritos, Enchiladas, and more. Scoop some onto a burger, or mix it with sour cream and mayo or yogurt for a crowd-pleasing dip!

What You'll Need

- 6 T. Go-Go Green Chile Spice Blend
- 4 cups chicken stock
- 1 T. fresh or 1 t. dried oregano
- 4 t. butter or vegetable oil (can substitute bacon grease for extra flavor)
- 2 onions, finely chopped
- 4-6 cloves of garlic, finely chopped (I like mine extra garlicky)
- 2 T. flour

How to Prepare

1. Heat oil over medium heat in a skillet or sauce pan.

2. Sautee onion and garlic for until onion is translucent.

3. Add Go-Go Green Chile Powder, oregano, and flour; mix thoroughly.

4. Add chicken stock in small batches; be sure to keep stirring so you don't end up with lumpy sauce!

5. Bring to a boil, then reduce heat and simmer for 15-20 minutes, stirring frequently. The longer it simmers the thicker the sauce will become.

6. Let cool, then use in your favorite recipes.

7. You can store this sauce in the refrigerator for 4-5 days, or freeze in small batches for later use.

Easy-Peasy
Go-Go Green Chile
Corn Salsa

This simple, yet surprisingly tasty corn salsa can be served on its own as an appetizer or side dish. You can also use it to top burgers or hot dogs, or as a unique addition to sandwiches and wraps. Another idea is to serve the salsa on small Romaine lettuce leaves for a colorful appetizer or party food.

Try it; you'll like it and chances are you'll discover new ways to enjoy it!

What You'll Need

- 1 package frozen or one 15-16 oz. can corn (buy a salt-free can if you can find it)
- ¼ cup fresh cilantro, finely chopped
- ¼ cup Bermuda onion, finely chopped

- Juice of ½ lemon
- 1-2 T. Go-Go Green Chile Spice Blend

How to Prepare

1. Open canned corn and drain well

   OR

   Cook frozen corn according to package directions; let cool.

2. In a glass or plastic bowl, mix corn, cilantro, onion, lemon juice, and Go-Go Green Chile.

3. Cover bowl and refrigerate for at least 30 min. This salsa will last a couple of days in the refrigerator, and will only taste better the longer the ingredients have a chance to blend together!

A Few Other Uses for Go-Go Green Chile Spice Blend

Eggs

- Mix in scrambled eggs
- Use in omelets
- Mix with egg before stirring into fried rice

Meats and Seafood

- Coat beef, chicken, pork, or seafood liberally before grilling, pan-frying, or roasting
- Sprinkle liberally on chicken wings before baking
- Mix with flour and bread crumbs to create a seasoned coating for baked pork chops or chicken wings

- Use in beer batter for fish, shrimp, or other fried seafood

Soups

- Sprinkle liberally in soups and stews while cooking
- Used to season meats, seafood, tofu, etc. before browning when making soups and stews

Casseroles

- Sprinkle liberally in macaroni and cheese sauce before mixing with pasta, then sprinkle more on top

Breads

- Mix in cornbread batter before baking

Use your imagination—the **possibilities are endless**!

And be sure to share your recipes on social media using the hashtag **#mountainmangourmet**!

Did you know?

*In New Mexico,
you can even order your Big Mac
with green chile!*

Order extra spice mixes today at:
http://mountainmangourmet.com!

48150710R00050

Made in the USA
San Bernardino, CA
19 April 2017